Flirting With Frogs

(Because sometimes your Prince takes longer than expected)

Maxie Marcell

Flirting With Frogs is a work of nonfiction. Some names and identifying details have been changed.

ISBN: 1507842236
ISBN 13: 9781507842232

Dedication

To the best role models in my life: my parents. You have shown me the meaning of true love and for that I have lived knowing that "happily ever after" really can come true. Thank you for taking me to Disney World all those years and letting me pretend I am one of the princesses. I am not lucky, I am blessed.

Most importantly to my husband- for showing me you love me every day and for feeding me snacks because you know it makes me happy. It is because of you I was able to finish this book with a happy ending. I always knew someday my prince would come (you just took longer than I would have liked). I love you always.

"Always wear your invisible crown"
-Anonymous

To: Mr & Mrs Juliano,
Thank you for your support!
Enjoy the book! Love you!
♡ Meshan/Maxie

I really overcommitted on my bad decisions.

This is what I used to think to myself as I sat alone in my room, usually with the lights off, reminiscing about lost loves. I would wonder how the person staring back at me in the mirror (thankfully that person was myself, not a ghost or Freddy Krueger) had such ridiculously low standards yet absurdly high expectations.

A few years ago I was a delusional girl trying to figure out why my love affairs always turned into self-torture miniseries. I was confident I knew exactly what I wanted and needed when it came to love, but every time I embarked on my love quest, I returned only with gremlins and goblins instead of a prince or Ryan Gosling.

As I dug deeper to find out why this continuously happened, I was able to come up with two explanations:

My Fairy Godmother is a drunk

Or

You can't find true love if you yourself are lost. When you love and respect yourself first, everything else will fall into place.

Clearly I went with the first choice since that was most logical, but needless to say I had a lot of soul searching to do.

"Trust me; I know I am a Disney Princess."

When I was growing up (hell, I'm still growing up) all I wanted was to fall in love and live happily ever after just like the Disney Princesses did.

Let's face it- those bitches had it made. Muscular, rich men in tights- usually born into royalty but hot one hundred percent of the time, flying dragons-or even better- flying humans, long luscious hair that ALWAYS looks good (whether asleep for a hundred years or casually living under the sea), tiny waists and majestic singing everywhere! Everyone just sings. Oh, you're a broom? No problem, you have the voice of an angel. Animals? Well of course they can sing, and they are adorable while doing it. Life could not have been better for them. Who would ever turn down the opportunity to sing with the birds and the bears while twirling about in a custom gown designed by mice? No one.

I should have known romance was not going to be that easy. I went to my first movie at the ripe age of four with my dad, otherwise known as the best man in the world. You know what movie it was? Beauty and the Beast. Freakin' classic. You know what I did? I started crying and screaming when the Beast "died" and transformed back into the human prince. This was supposed to be a joyous and magical moment, but not for me it wasn't. I wanted that gigantic, hairy, cape-wearing werewolf to come back and dance with Belle in the snow. WHY COULDN'T EVERYONE LEAVE THEM ALONE?

My dad didn't know what to do at this point. I think he just laughed and pretended that his daughter wasn't this tiny weirdo. Whatever. That prince was so much better as a grumpy, ballroom dancing buffalo and everyone knows it.

As I have gotten older I wonder: was this a foreshadowing to how future dating life would be? Quite possibly so. Or maybe I just had issues...still trying to figure that one out.

How foolish of me to think that the fairytales of my childhood could become a reality. I'll admit I was pretty pissed when I hit puberty and there were no boys, let alone princes, kissing me as I woke up in the morning nor were there birds fluttering about my room hanging up my clothes. I couldn't throw pixie dust into the air and fly off to Neverland to escape from responsibility. Oh, and I came to the soul-crushing realization that you should never, under any circumstances, try to sing with animals-mainly the bears...because you will die. That's a fact.

I had serious questions that demanded answers. Someone needed to explain why princes didn't exist in America, not to mention why they weren't lined up outside my door. There were approximately zero handsome gentlemen searching the lands for me as I sat in bed binge watching Sex and the City. I could have sworn that being bed-ridden was a requirement in order to get a man (oh, how I wish this were true) and now the world was proving differently? On top of that, I have to physically put my own clothes away and be, like, responsible? AND I CAN'T EVEN SING NICE? Fuck this. What is this travesty of a life?

This made me question my entire childhood and all I ever knew to be true. The only thing that translated over in real life were the men in tights—but come to find out they were never going to be interested in me. Who knew?

Once I got over the fact I had to settle for everyday common folk, I began to date. And boy did I date. I like to try to experience all the world has to offer me, you know? I spent most days of my younger adult years pushing way too hard in all the wrong places to find love. It was literally all I thought about and I only made it worse by believing in every love story I saw in a movie or read about in a book. I would meet guys, give them every benefit of the doubt, ignore the red flags, start a relationship, watch it quickly torpedo to the ground, be sad, get back up, brush it off and repeat. And so it went.

Leonardo da Vinci knew what he was talking about when he said, "Life without love is no life at all" but I think he left out a couple minor details. One main point being that while a life with love may be a divine slice of heaven, it can also be the literal inferno Dante himself trudged through. Am I right?

I will preface this book by saying that no, this story does not begin with "Once upon a time," but it does include some dragons, fairy godmothers, a blonde chick who is eternally convinced she is a royal princess (me), and tales of failed relationships proving to everyone that life would be so much better if we lived in a Disney movie.

"The Boyfriend Box"

I am fairly confident that most adolescents had one of these. Whether it's called the "boyfriend box" or the "box of lies," we all know what it is. I was thirteen years old when I decided to start mine. By this I mean taking an empty Sketchers shoe box and filling it with crap from boyfriends past. There was also a top secret document listing all the characteristics I absolutely needed in a boyfriend. How else was I supposed to know what kind of guy I wanted? The list was everything.

Isn't this still how it goes today? We meet someone and instantly start sizing them up and scrolling down the good ol' checklist:

- Taller than me-Frodo Baggins not welcome
- A smile that won't turn me to stone
- Kind to everyone (mostly me)
- Does he bring out my fake laugh or real laugh
- Can we hold a decent conversation or do I want to rip every strand of hair out
- Solid brain power
- Goal oriented...which, as you get older, eventually turns into: employed (this should probably be at the top)

- Single. Because of course we will always have to worry about this
- Offers me food and beverages...a lot.

And if we are lucky enough to meet someone with at least three characteristics off our list (preferably the last one), it's game on.

My first serious diagnosis of "boy crazy" was when I was in the eighth grade. At a young age, I was already bored with the ordinary ways of dating. This was mainly because I knew nothing about dating. So because I like to shoot for the stars, I became infatuated with an older man. He was a junior in high school and also happened to be my cousin's best friend.

Oh the drama of it all.

I needed him. He had me acting like an obsessive One Direction groupie. But, you know what's crazy? From the minute we met (I was *basically* 14) I know he felt something too. Yes, I realize that is bordering on creepy, Woody Allen pedophile status, but it wasn't like that. It was genuine and sweet; a connection you don't encounter too often in life.

You know what's even crazier? After a little determination and a lot of patience, we actually ended up dating when I became a freshman in high school. My fairytale seemed to be starting right on time and I sat there believing that by some act of magic, I had been chosen for the next classic romance.

Were my dreams coming true at such a young age? Could I be so lucky?

Alright...so my fairytale reveries were slightly premature. Our courtship didn't last—I knew it was doomed the second he handed me my first love note...written in some sort of Egyptian coding system. You think I am joking, but unfortunately I speak the truth. For some reason we had to do this so no one could see what we were saying...therefore numbers were substituted for letters and I then had to decipher the message like it was the god damn Da Vinci Code.

As he was on the brink of ending a big milestone (high school), I was just starting mine and that was ultimately why it didn't last. Our two worlds just never fit together regardless of how much we cared about each other. We were simply two good people with bad timing. Minus our differences, I could not have picked a better gentleman to kick off my dating extravaganzas.

The moral of this story is that if you believe in something enough, and if you stay true to yourself, then you can have the world...and hieroglyphic notes. #dreambig

After that relationship, I lived out my high school days as if I was a four year contestant on the Dating Game- throwing out I love you's like they were free t-shirts at a basketball game.

The world of dating changed for me when I entered college. I was somewhat sheltered (in a good way) growing up, so being on my own was both awakening and terrifying, I was now learning to: become more independent, make friends with bouncers so my under aged ass could get into bars, shamelessly eat pizza for breakfast, lunch, and dinner, and consume (what seemed like) hundreds of shots in a row while managing to function in class the next day. I was alive and winning at life.

It was during my second semester as a college freshman when I met my first "frog" and started my descent through the dating abyss. Before I was able to run to the light, I had to crawl in the dark with these five.

Let the modern day fairy tale begin. Buckle up bitches.

"Cinderella never asked for a Prince. She asked for a night off and a dress."

-Kiera Cass

The Cheater

He didn't change for the person before you, he won't change for you, and he will never change for the one after you. A man is who he is. If he's a snake, he'll always be a snake. No matter how hard you try to avoid them, you usually end up loving at least one.

First loves...they are kind of inescapable, like a black hole. I was eighteen and didn't know any better, so naturally I fell for an older, handsome, blue-eyed boy. Not because I was slightly intoxicated when we first met, but because I enjoyed scraping guys off the bottom of the barrel and then dating them.

We met at a college bar. I was visiting friends and he was doing the same. I know...super romantic, just like how I dreamed it would be. We met, we drank, we kissed, we danced, and we exchanged numbers. Typical Saturday night if you ask me, only to my surprise he actually called the next day.

To give you an idea of how incredibly low my standards were, I thought the gesture of his call was literally the sweetest thing ever; man of the year award in my book. Look Dad, I am raising the bar just like you said!

He pursued me in a way every woman should be pursued. I was smitten and with the snap of a finger we started to feel all the feels which led us into a serious relationship. I mean, I at least thought it was a serious relationship. Those exist right?

My heart was wide open-beating to the rhythm of this new love. I thought he was the best thing that could ever enter my little lonely life. The relationship was easy and mature...it just worked. It seemed like the answers to my prayers finally came true.

He told me he loved me first. I said it back and meant it with all I had. He knew I loved him more. After that he became my "first" for a few things...the sneaky little bastard. We would spend hours talking about our future- picking out dogs, where we wanted to live and how many kids we were going to have. I was in love and totally annoying about it.

God I know I was so annoying.

The honeymoon stage is always the best, isn't it? You enter this gigantic cloud of oblivion and false hope; drifting away and making everyone hate you and your never-ending, idiotic smile. Those were the days. Sadly, what goes up must come down. There you are floating around in your happy place until one day your cloud decides to shit on you. Reality crashes down on the very world you live in—similar to the way Miley Cyrus crashed in on that wrecking ball (except hopefully you are clothed when it happens).

I will sum this up quick: it was a delicious seventy-five degree summer day. The breeze was blowing through my golden hair and aside from my sweat mustache; I looked banging in my Abercrombie denim skirt and white tank. We were at one of Drew's (that is what we will call him) softball games and I couldn't be more ready to watch my man play some ball.

Soon he would be up to bat, so Drew asked if I would hold onto his wallet and cell phone. I placed the items carefully inside my oversized Guess bag (is Guess even still relevant?) while giving a reassuring glance as if to say, "don't worry sweetie, your possessions are safe with me."

I gave myself approximately five seconds to pretend that I was truly enjoying the game and not thinking, in any way, about looking through his phone. I couldn't help myself. You know that feeling; that curiosity, eating away at you. It was burning a hole through my bag, begging me to take one quick peek. So I did. Obviously I went straight for the messages.

#sorrynotsorry

He never gave me reason to doubt him, but I knew I was going to find something; I had that gut feeling. Usually the only gut feeling I experience is hunger, but this felt different. I should have put my trust in my loving boyfriend and wipe out any negative thoughts, but I am just way too nosey and refuse to let anyone make a fool out of me.

I casually skimmed through the inbox and nothing of interest caught my eye. Once that check was complete, I ventured over to the sent messages. Remember when text messages were separated into sent/received folders? I opened the sent folder and BAM: eyes were bleeding...immediate regret.

At this point I would have been OK with a giant lightning bolt striking me down to my death. Sexting? Who even sexted in those days?! Do you want to know how I knew Drew was an idiot? Because he was so confident he had his shit covered, by deleting all of his inbox messages, but somehow forgot to delete his sent texts. Do I look like an amateur to you? If you are going to play games, honey, you best believe you need to cover all your bases. These hazel eyes miss nothing.

It was the bitch slap I never saw coming. Was I being punked? Maybe I misunderstood the message, "you make me so horny." Maybe they were, like, quoting Austin Powers or something. Or maybe he was typing too fast and autocorrect assumed he was trying to say those words. Autocorrect can be a real smartass sometimes.

I left the bleachers for a second because I was choking on reality. In my hour of despair, I found myself in a porter potty. That's right- a feces infested heat box. How much lower can one get on a Saturday?

Naturally I called my best friend and she wanted to come pick me up right then and there. She tried so hard to talk me into leaving because she is a good friend and that's what friends do, but I stayed. I stayed and wallowed in my misery until I could get some answers. To this day, I hate that I stayed.

The game finally ends after what seemed like forty-five innings and Drew comes over to me, sees my face and has the audacity to ask me what's wrong.

Oh, does it seem like something's wrong? I mean, besides the terror I experienced in the porter potty and the distasteful texts I had the pleasure of reading on your phone, I am really having a lovely afternoon. Tea anyone?

Rage was coursing through my veins and on the inside I was screaming. I looked him dead in the eyes and confronted him about the texts. Like a professional sleaze ball, he had the quickest, calmest explanation. Drew told me the texts were a joke with a friend who lives out of state and meant nothing.

Are. You. Fucking. Kidding. Me.

What kind of trickery is this? What is this fire you spit at me? I read your messages to another girl about wanting to do inappropriate things and you get to sit there and tell me it's just a joke and that's it?

Well, yes. That was it. It was as if he knew he had to be prepared to explain himself and honestly, he did it so well. "I love you" poured out of his mouth every chance he got and he made me feel like I was the only girl in the entire world for him. He said he would never do anything like that again and I ate it up. He said he loved me and wanted to be with me forever and I believed every word. He said he would make it up to me and show me I can always trust him and so, of course, I let him.

I wish the me I am now could have smacked some sense into the me I was then. Now that I am older, it's clear that all of this had to happen. I was so naïve and lived in this nice little place where people meant what they said. I never imagined someone would ever wrong me like that. It's a story most of us know all too well: We accept. We ignore. We turn our heads for the sake of love.

Time went on and so did we, but not as we once were. I hated the person I was becoming. I felt like I had to always be on guard and those messages kept dancing in my head on repeat.

However, there came a day when I finally got a bone thrown my way. The scene looked like this: Drew and I were hanging out at his house and he had to go drop off a video to a guy he coached basketball with. I declined to tag along because I am lazy and "Friends" was on. Like, hello, did you really think I would stop watching "Friends" to go run an errand? What do you take me for?

As soon as he left, I had an overwhelming urge to snoop around. Who wouldn't? While I was on my little adventure, I stumbled upon a small notebook inside a desk drawer. I flipped through and came across a page titled, "Drew's Passwords." The Holy Grail. It was like that notebook was waiting to be found by yours truly. Just so I am clear, this was a list of every single one of his passwords-to EVERYTHING. I took this discovery as a gift; a sign from above if you will.

You know in those horror movies where the main character is trying to either unlock a door or start a car before the killer gets to them? This entire experience was pretty much like that. My hands wrote in a speed that has never been seen before and I marveled in my small accomplishment before Drew got home.

For the record, to this day, he never found out that I did this. Well, until probably right now.

You would think this was how I found out he was physically cheating on me, but that is not the case. Checking his Facebook and email started to become like a second job; it was constant and I couldn't stop. At times it put my mind to ease, but I just knew there was something I was not seeing. At the same time he was treating me like gold which made things even more confusing. I loved him with all my heart, but was living in a trust-less relationship and wasn't strong enough to follow the exit signs yet.

THE BREAKUP

The randomness of how I found out still boggles my mind to this day. This is living proof that what goes around, always comes back around. Say it with me: Karma is a bitch.

Here is how it went down:

It was day one of my college spring break and I had plans to go to New York City with my friend later that week. Around ten in the morning I received a phone call from one of my girlfriends telling me Drew had been cheating on me.

Um, can you not? Could I enjoy one day of vacation? My mom and I had a full day of shopping planned which was all ruined because my slut boyfriend couldn't keep it in his pants.

After one receives such crucial information, it is only natural to do all necessary research and gather every single detail so you are properly prepared for battle. First, I needed to find out where this information came from.

Prepare for your minds to be blown.

This girl we both went to high school with was currently attending college hours away from home. She was having a pow wow session with her friends and some random girls and, as most women do, were sharing gossip about relationships and probably discussing politics over bagels and breakfast burritos. You know... the normal life of a college student.

Well, one chick started divulging details about how her friend has been seeing this guy, Drew, but he has a girlfriend and the friend wants to give him an ultimatum. It's either her or the pathetic girlfriend.

Oh. Is that so?

The girl I went to high school with confirmed Drew's full name with the random chick just to be sure. Clearly I had some friends in high places who didn't want to allow this bullshit into my life any longer.

I am not going to lie...it was painful; excruciatingly painful. This was my very first love who I truly thought I would spend the rest of my life with. Nothing is worse than knowing you are not enough for someone.

As soon as I heard the words "he is cheating on you" I had no doubt in my mind that they were true. Isn't that sad?

I stood motionless in my room for a while, not really knowing what to do. I could tell my mom's heart was breaking for me and if it were up to her, Drew would have magically disappeared without a trace. Forever. Bippity boppity boo.

The fact that Drew was working all day made everything worse. How was I supposed to wait hours with this information weighing heavy on my soul? Patience is not a strong virtue of mine. Instead of sitting around in agony, my mom and I did the one thing that always, no matter what the circumstance, makes us feel better: we went shopping.

After an eternity of waiting and trying to distract myself with shoes and clothing, Drew arrived home and it was time to make my move. I briefly thought about driving my car into oncoming traffic, but then decided I needed to handle my problem. My mom always used to tell me: you either handle your problem or the problem handles you and that is some of the best advice I have ever been given. I'll be honest and say that part of me wanted to handle this problem by digging a hole in the dirt and disposing of Drew's body, but I didn't have time for that kind of work.

I couldn't let him get away with what he did to me. He should have never underestimated my ability to find shit out. Little did he know I have minions everywhere to tell me all his secrets.

Those that are scorned are to be most feared.

I went to the door. It opened. He tried to kiss me with his stupid face. NOPE. Touch me and die. He asked me what's wrong. I could barely look at him. He knows I know. Things got awkward.

Being the smart person that I am, I didn't give away all my knowledge of the situation at once. He thought he could play games, so I played one too. This, I soon learned, was a good lesson for many life situations.

As expected, Drew first tried acting like he had no idea what I was talking about. Next, he said he only knew her from a volleyball team they both play on. Then he proceeded to say they never hung out. The more details I revealed, the more flustered he got. It didn't take long for him to start talking, but even then he still wasn't fully honest. With his tail between his legs, he admitted they kissed...but only once. Oh, but promised it would never happen again.

Cross your heart and hope to die? It was half of a confession.

I would say this is the about the time I entered the ninth circle of hell. As one can imagine, it is not exactly considered a vacation destination-I do not recommend it to others. The truth, or at least some of it, eventually came out and kissing was the least of it- they slept together. How many times I will never know nor do I care to but he had now started a war he would never win.

After everything was laid out on the table like Thanksgiving dinner, I was immediately drowning in apology phone calls and texts. He cried and begged for forgiveness and I just stayed in bed, also crying and begging for this nightmare to end.

The only positive that came out of all of this was that for the first (and only) time in my life I wasn't hungry. Talk about a great weight loss plan. I wish I could bottle that up and sell it-instant millionaire.

After the breakup, there were sporadic conversations, mostly consisting of him trying to get me back. I considered the idea for one millisecond, but realized I couldn't put myself through that. If the person I am with can't respect me the way I respect myself then it will never work.

You can't build a relationship without a strong foundation and there is no foundation without trust.

It takes some serious, con artist type skill to make your girlfriend believe you are madly in love with her while maintaining a side piece at the same time. Bravo, you clown; you tricked us all. If there was a trophy for world's biggest douchebag, it would surely be in a glass case with your name on it.

It will never cease to amaze me how mystifying time can truly be. It has been over eight years and I found myself recently sitting at a bar directly across from Drew, who was now a perfect stranger to me. At one time, many, many moons ago, this person was the center of my universe; I built countless dreams around this man. But as I looked at him (still had a stupid face), I felt nothing towards him- not anger, not hate, not anything. The opposite of love is indifference and that is exactly how I felt. I don't know anything about that person anymore, in fact most of the time I forget he exists. That is the power of time and that is why life always goes on.

Thank you Fairy Godmother.

"All I ask is that you treat me no differently than you would the Queen."

-Anonymous

The Missing Link

As I continued on in my search for love it appeared I had to make another stop. He wasn't my prince, but he happened to be just what I needed at the time.

Some people are sent into your life at just the right moment- whether you thought you needed them or not. Sometimes all we need is that teddy bear to hold onto to let us know everything will be alright. Corey was my teddy bear, proving that good guys still do exist.

Let's take a walk down memory lane, shall we?

Plant this thought in your head: young college girl meets cute, older bouncer- totally not cliché whatsoever. I had the biggest crush on this guy before I even met Drew. I was eighteen which meant I was at the prime of my "cool years." During my first year of college, I thought just as much about going out and meeting boys as I did about classes. Don't most single girls?

(I am making my parents so proud right now)

There were the typical college bars we were allowed access to—the ones who pretend every college kid is of legal drinking age so they can still make money. Fortunately for me, I didn't panic when it came to going out; from what I could tell, I had the nightlife scene under control. Fake identification was, like, the way of the 2000's anyway- everyone had one. It didn't matter that my ID portrayed me as a twenty-eight year old blonde with a face that looked like she did hard time.

There was one bar in particular that my friends and I frequented and over the course of our first semester, we began to see the same faces and buddy up to the bartenders and bouncers, who are always important people to know. One Saturday night my girls and I made our way out, ready to take down the night. As our heels were clicking on the polluted sidewalks of Main Street and our scarcely dressed bodies were experiencing the beginning phases of hypothermia, we were ready to party. We inched closer to our "hangout" when we realized our usual bouncer companion was nowhere to be seen. He was our trusted man-friend who knew we were undercover children and let us in anyway. That is what friendship is all about people.

Our walk slowed as our eyes frantically searched for that familiar face. Another minute passed and we still couldn't locate him-completely unacceptable on his part. There was no way we were going to turn around and go home so we decided to take our chances; after all it was just a club, not Buckingham Palace.

A larger, scarier looking man came into view and he was guarding the front door like he was Attila the Hun. I was thinking that one of two things would happen: Attila would be like, "oh these girls are the most adorable things I have ever laid eyes on-they are welcome any time" or "who let these twelve year olds in miniskirts out unsupervised?"

Thankfully, my friends each got in with their IDs and then it was my turn. Just so you know, I am about as smooth as a cheese grater. My talent is taking an uncomfortable situation and bringing it to a whole new level of uncomfortable. With that said, I marched right up to the front of the line with my fake confidence in hand and all I managed to get out was a Mrs. Doubtfire, "helloooooo!"

This officially just got mortifying.

Isn't it amazing how you can bring the smallest clutch you own yet still can't manage to find anything? It's like you are digging through Mary Poppins tote. "Oh, silly me, that's not my ID that's just a lamp. One moment...let me reach back in here..."

Of freaking course I could not find my fake ID. I obnoxiously tried to stall time by letting out a weird laugh and saying something embarrassing like "oh God, this always happens to me! I am so sorry I don't know where I could have placed that thing..." But in my head I was like, "End me now."

Corey couldn't be less interested in my charm. He was there for one simple reason and showed no mercy while doing it. He just stood there; giving zero fucks about my struggle...such a monster.

I was running out of excuses when suddenly, as if he descended from the skies above, my bouncer friend came to my rescue. Praise the good Lord. I made sure to flash a "how do you like me now" smile at Corey as I walked in.

The night carried on as usual and I didn't think twice about Corey, after all I was pretty sure he thought I was a degenerate. I had plans to never speak to him again, but unfortunately for me there is always a point in the night where one must excuse herself to get some fresh air. This comes from living out the words, "dance like no one is watching" to the most literal meaning and I am not a graceful sweater.

As I was positioning my body in the best direction to catch the night breeze, Corey actually started speaking to me instead of standing there and passing judgment. This man that terrified me earlier was actually just one big teddy bear and yes, I wanted to squeeze him. Strange how my perception of him quickly changed with a little conversation. We hit it off in the friendliest way possible and by the end of the night I somehow left with his number (most likely my unforgiving charm) and the next thing I knew we were texting.

Did I just grow a set of balls? I have never casually asked for someone's number before. I was officially a bro.

There were occasional phone conversations and I saw him once a week...at the bar. I was at the age where the mystery of the unknown was enticing. The friendly flirtations were a fun little game; the thrill of the chase. These shenanigans went on for months and our pillow talks became my new bedtime routine. Did I also mention that Corey was seven years older than me? Minor, minor detail.

Looking back now, I know that I was too available...actually, I was *always* available. I would answer every time he called. Couldn't I have at least pretended to have other things going on? I was the late night booty call minus the booty. During the day, there was no communication, but when the sun had set I became the woman of the night. We would chat for hours until dawn and the entire time I would secretly hold my breath, hoping he would ask me out on a date.

Do you like me or not, man? Take a girl out. FEED ME. Do I look like I want to be pen pals? Do you think I am giving up precious hours of my beauty sleep each night for my health? The more time that went by without a date, the more frustrated I became. Needless to say the whole "thrill of the chase" thing became downright exhausting. I was no longer thrilled. What man only has an interest in talking on the phone? A girl can only wait for so long and then we have to take matters into our own hands. I was over it and made the executive decision to cut off communication.

Corey would text me randomly and all conversation eventually dwindled. I would see him on an occasional Saturday night but mostly kept my distance. Not too long after that whole scene I met Drew...and we all know how that went down.

The hysterical thing was that as soon as Corey heard I had a boyfriend, he thought I made it up in an effort to make him jealous. Ok no, honey. You are great, but you are no Gerard Butler, so get over yourself. I think my jaw hit the floor when he looked me in the face and told me (with major attitude) that he had wanted to hang out all that time. Excuse moi? Am I some sort of game to you? The only game I will ever be is fucking battleship. He should have known that Beyoncé taught me better than that and so to the left, to the left he went.

That is the backstory on how I met Corey. This is when the real story began:

Remember how I had plans to go to New York City on my spring break during my sophomore year (the spring break that was ultimately destroyed because I found out Drew was cheating on me with some slob)? Well, I went on that trip with my girlfriend and it just so happened to be the place where Corey was residing. I contacted him as soon as we landed in the Big Apple and also made him aware of my newly single status.

Don't you just love how some things work out?

Just because I was not looking for anything, didn't mean I couldn't use some distraction. Corey happened to be my perfect target.

Seeing him face to face had my stomach tangled up like Rapunzel's hair. Excitement had been nothing but a lost emotion for me and yet at that moment I felt it. My friend and I met his group at a pub, which of course was swimming with people. I spotted him right away and he looked exactly like how I remembered him.

The look on his face when he saw me was priceless; he was genuinely happy to see me and the feeling was mutual. Once Corey elbowed his way through what seemed like hundreds of people, we embraced- both surprised we were actually hanging out like this. It was as if all my worries flew out the window; a sense of ease fell over me and I was ready to go wherever the night decided to take me.

Mixed drinks were flowing, music was blaring, and I was having way too much fun putting St. Patrick's Day stickers all over my face. For a few hours I was able to forget the asshole that broke me. So cheers to me. It was a night that was well deserved.

Of course it was music to Cory's ears knowing I was single again and he made sure to shower me with affection. I can't say that I disliked it, but it didn't feel right. My heart and mind were in a land far, far away as I was still digesting what happened days earlier, but after the way I had been feeling the past few days, it felt damn good to be wanted.

We stayed out all night and I actually had *fun*. After our bar hopping extravaganza, we dragged our bodies to IHOP-the place where dreams come true. There was so much goodness being shoveled into my face that for a minute I swore I had entered the gates of heaven. Satisfied with the meals we just conquered, my girlfriend and I decided to crash at Corey's apartment because there was no way in hell we would have figured out how to get back to our hotel in New Jersey on our own.

The next day we kept it simple: I headed back home and he said he would call (stop getting all excited, nothing happened the night before). Simple was good. Simple worked.

Corey called every day, even when the sun was still out, and it slowly helped me move on. Our conversations were lighthearted and fun and I was able to start looking towards the future instead of dwelling on the past. The fact that we lived in different cities lifted the pressure of things moving too quickly.

I believe Corey knew I was still damaged from my breakup, but I don't think he knew the extent of it and I wasn't about to be that annoying loon who constantly talks about my sad feelings. No one wants to be dragged through someone else's mud. I needed to put my big girl panties on (if I could find any without cartoons or cupcakes on them) and move forward. All you can really do is try.

Round and around we went on our favorite merry-go-round. His feelings grew deeper and I was an idiot because I still couldn't commit. I have a hard enough time choosing what I want for dinner, so trying to make a decision on whether or not I should jump into a long distance relationship was beyond difficult. I knew I was sending mixed signals; half of me wanted the same things he did, but the other half needed space and wanted to be free. To be or not to be, that was the fucking question.

Unfortunately, we had more issues than just geography. In no way am I a needy chick, but a girl does like attention every now and then. I was getting nada. Zilch. Corey was a bit of a workaholic and there would be times I would barely hear from him all day or where he would call and mainly talk about work. Uh, no. Tell me nice things about myself. Tell me you miss me. TELL ME I'M PRETTY!!

To try to move things forward, Corey decided to visit me. I remember being both nervous and excited to have him come to my house...or should I say my parents' house. Let's be serious I was not an independent person at that time. We were taking one giant leap (for mankind) and hoping for the best and I could finally show my parents that he was a real human being.

This is where I'm supposed to tell you how he swooped in and rescued me from my loneliness and sorrow and became my real life Prince Charming. Well, I am sorry to inform you that none of that happened. Because why would it?

First I need to get this out of the way: we went to Friday's...as in TGI Friday's. There is no shade being thrown at Friday's, I always love me a good soup and breadsticks combo, not to mention the brownie obsession is literally the eighth wonder of the world, but I just figured for a first "date" we would maybe step it up a notch. This date was a big deal! I mean, I ate a mound of french fries and guzzled down more Diet Pepsi's than any human should ever be allowed to consume.

Maybe you are thinking, "Ok so she went to Friday's. Stop being a snooty bitch; it's about the company not the scenery" and I get that. Everyone is entitled to an opinion, but TGI Friday's is for jeans and hoodie wearing couples who have been dating for over two years and want to have a date night, but are too lazy to go anywhere farther than five miles from home. This was not that type of date- we had nice clothes on and I even put on heels.

To top that off, I also had to compete for attention with his cell phone, a Blackberry no less. You couldn't even download an app at the time-talk about humiliation. Was I that boring? Was he playing and intense game of solitaire? Did the video he downloaded finally start playing after taking two days to load? We never saw each other and I had better conversation with the waiter about how I wanted my burger cooked. We should have just Skyped. At least then I could have sat cross legged in sweatpants. The worst thing about it was that I never even got to order the brownie obsession. What a catastrophe.

Dinner ended and we decided to go see Shrek (another classic). The cell phone fiasco not only lasted through dinner, but carried on into the movie as well. People on their cellphones during a movie make my skin crawl. How do you even do that? It is almost physically impossible to be in a bad mood during Shrek, but it happened. Shrek had been compromised.

It may have been the texting, or it may have been the fact that I was clearly not ready for anything serious that drove me away-probably a combination of both. I barricaded myself with distance and didn't know how to explain it to him.

I am being really nice to myself right now. The truth is I was young, immature, and not ready...simple as that.

Slowly but surely I once again disappeared and so did the communication. Days turned into weeks, but then in the month of September I performed my very own Houdini act and reappeared. It was Corey's birthday and yes, I was thinking of him. "Happy birthday" was the cool, yet easygoing text I sent him and about two minutes later my phone rang.

We immediately fell back into our old routine like nothing had happened. Ok, so maybe I was being a little selfish. There was a small part of me that was happy to know that he still had feelings for me. Maybe it was a little cruel and unfair on my part, but I did care about him and was trying to see if maybe this time the feelings would be mutual. I wanted him in my life.

I wasn't giving up on this relationship yet, so I decided that I would make one last attempt to see if we could truly make it work. I booked a flight to visit Corey. A combo pack of anxious, excited, and scared raced through my body as I boarded the plane. Anxious because I didn't fully comprehend what in the hell I was doing. Excited because I had no idea what in the hell I was doing. And scared because I still had no idea what in the hell I was doing.

He picked me up from the airport and we spent most of our time catching up, laughing, sightseeing and eating. The perfect day was coming to an end when I realized I overlooked one detail- sleeping arrangements. Uneasiness flooded over me. I wanted to lock myself in the bathroom and smash my face into the mirror. Was I even for real right now? I couldn't believe I was remotely feeling this way. I flew all this way to visit a man I cared about and now I wanted to run for the hills?

Oh God what did I get myself in to? Why didn't humans come equipped with a panic button? I was so nervous and started to plan an exit strategy. Do I pretend to pass out really quick? Do I fake a stomach ache? Do I just let whatever happens, happen? The moment arrives where we get into bed and nope, I do not want it. We chatted for a couple minutes and he kissed me and then I mumbled something lame about being tired from the busy day and went to sleep.

That, my friends, is how you serve a double dose of awkward.

The next night was an even taller glass of awkward. We went out with a bunch of his friends: lots of drinking, dancing and more drinking. Now, I wasn't drunk at all for whatever reason, but I needed to be. The only game plan in place at that point was to start pretending I was drunk so I could "pass out" when we got back to his apartment. And that's exactly what I did. Maybe acting should be my next career move?

The rest of the trip went fine, but I was looking forward to getting home. I was disappointed. The weekend left me feeling the complete opposite of how I imagined and those few short days helped me come to the conclusion that love cannot be forced.

Corey got the hint that I couldn't make that jump and at the end of the day we lived in different states. We would have been setting ourselves up for failure. It was the tale of two people of different ages and different places, both physically and emotionally.

It was an amicable split and I still wish him nothing but the very best. Some people you just need in your life to pick you up when you have fallen down and that is exactly what Corey did for me in many ways.

He was a good man, just the wrong man.

"Life is not a fairytale. If you lose your shoe at midnight, you're drunk."

-Unknown

The Almost Lover

Before you dive into this one, you may want to get out a bottle of wine. This is the part where I took the wrong turn, drank the bad potion, ate the poison apple, etc.

Welcome to the never-ending story of my life; the saga that was always left at "to be continued. "So get comfortable, put your fat pants on, keep your arms and legs inside the moving vehicle and enjoy the ride.

This type of guy may seem familiar- he barges into your life unannounced and unexpected. He's a mental hurricane who goes against everything you thought you wanted. He's the one you hate and then you love. He's unconventional. He's Sebastian.

Nothing grinds my gears harder than people who file their relationship status as "it's complicated. "I viciously judge those kinds of people. Why is that option even available to us? Can you not make up your minds? Relationships were always black and white to me- you're either with someone or you're not. You love them or you leave them. It's supposed to be easy, right?

On most normal days my belief is that relationships are that simple. When two people like each other, they make it happen and the rest is history. If you can't make it happen then what is the point? Gift wrap it in shiny paper, hand it to God, and move on.

There I was, traveling down my yellow brick road (red slippers included) when this character came along and dropped a house on me. It was my first experience entering the forbidden grey area of relationships (unfortunately not the fifty shades kind). "It's complicated" was the only way to classify this one.

The very first time I met Sebastian, I was dating Drew. Remember him? He's like a cockroach- never goes away. Coincidentally, back in the day Sebastian and Drew were the best of friends.

Hello again Karma, I see what you did there.

I remember the encounter: my initial thoughts of him were: loud, obnoxiously funny, and borderline crazy. I would barely consider us acquaintances since we only met a few times and since I was madly in love with my boyfriend of the year, he wasn't in my realm of thinking.

Seeing as how my original plan of spending the rest of my life with Drew went down in flames, I found myself back on the market. As I was settling into my single gal persona, I bumped into Sebastian at a local bar. Of course, just like everything else about him, our official "meet-cute" was anything but normal.

I was making my way out the door when Sebastian (who was also newly single) stumbled up to me, disregarding every aspect of my personal space. He placed his face uncomfortably close to mine and slurred something along the lines of, "I'm sorry about you and Drew. We both know he's an asshole. I know you loved him and he loved you back, but you'll be ok."

Is this supposed to be a pep talk? Thank you?

Call me crazy, but I could have sworn on the bible itself that Sebastian and Drew were good friends. Like, really good friends. What was happening here? He started flirting with me; it was happening right before my very eyes.

Is this a test?

Am I failing?

Why is he smiling like that at me?

Sebastian not only proceeded to tell me how attractive he thinks I am, but that he has always wanted to say that to me.

Hi, um...God? Are you up there? Can I be excused for the rest of my life please?

Sebastian asked for my number and knowing it was a horrible decision, I gave it to him anyway. I didn't even care anymore. I was a young lady on the mend which was enough justification for any actions that came to follow. Oh the sweet, sweet taste of revenge. I was basically gargling it.

I was walking blindly into this random yet interesting situation with Sebastian. After he got my number we had sporadic conversations and of course there were flirtations, but I had zero expectations. Usually by now a guy would be telling me "you're the one" and yet with Sebastian it was all very mysterious. But I knew I had to play it cool; I had to act like I was the one running our little game when in reality I didn't even know the game had started.

The beginning stages of this "relationship" was a bit like ping pong (without the Asian guys grunting back and forth): one minute things were strictly in the friend zone and the next extremely flirty. I was enjoying myself, but confused at where my love life was heading.

I was losing control of my emotions and the situation. I realized I needed to slap myself back to reality, regain composure of the situation, and remind myself, "You is kind, you is smart, you is important. "Words to live by; Aibileen Clark is an inspiration to us all. If you don't know what I am talking about, then we can't be friends.

This was my summer, dammit! I was single and ready to mingle; I was officially bringing mingling back. As soon as I was getting the hang of the flirtation game, Sebastian, in typical male fashion, had to go wreak havoc on everything.

A big birthday blowout-complete with a limo bus (does anything good ever come of these?) was planned for Sebastian. His friends, a bunch of my girlfriends, and I were invited and you would have thought we were teenagers at our first party. To my surprise, I didn't spend much time with Sebastian; he was actually getting rather cozy with this other girl I didn't know. I won't lie, I thought we would interact more since he had been texting me quite a bit, but Ok. You do you.

The following morning, while I was trying to put the pieces together from the night before, I received a text from Sebastian that sent me into a frenzy. The text said something along the lines of, "I know you like me and I like you, but I am going to have to play the Drew card-it just can't happen-so you're going to have to deal with it babe."

I'm sorry, what? On a scale of one to fucking never did he think it would be acceptable to wake me from my slumber with that nonsense? On a Sunday morning no less? Sunday is the SABBATH; a day of rest. How rude.

He must have still been drunk when he woke up. Either that or that "other girl" was so boring that he needed to find attention elsewhere. I just could not deal. Sebastian and his oversized ego needed to take a seat.

Not only was the text baffling, but it was confusing to the point where I had no idea what he was talking about. At first I had no response, which is rare for me. Are we five years old? Just to be clear sweetheart, I did not come after you- that was your move. You got my number remember? It was also painfully obvious that neither of us gave a shit about Drew.

This should have been a situation I just laughed off, but I was seeing red. My plate was already stacked with enough drama and I sure as hell didn't need anymore. Like an adult, I took a moment to collect my thoughts and then proceeded to let Sebastian know his accusations were undoubtedly false. Our text war was kept short; we were those two kids who couldn't play nice in the sandbox. *You better tread lightly...this is my sand, bitch!*

A week later my friends informed me that Sebastian and his roommate were having a party. Was I personally invited? No. Did I go anyway? Yes. Why? Because I do whatever the hell I want...A.K.A. every single one of my friends was going and I couldn't bear the thought of sitting home alone.

I knew what I had to do: look hot and kill him with kindness--I don't know if that is a thing, but it should be. So I put on a new face (makeup does wonders), shoved my body into a cute summer dress, prayed that I wouldn't sweat like a farm animal, and off I went.

I already knew how the night was going to go. Sebastian and I were going to pretend to avoid each other while making eye contact every five minutes. There would be exaggerated interest in random conversations we could really care less about all while keeping an eye on what the other was doing. Damn, that's exhausting. Talk about multi-tasking with your emotions.

The truth is, we both knew exactly what we were doing. It may not have been wanted or welcomed, but there was chemistry there. I don't know how or why it happened, but it did. Apparently I love inserting myself into disastrous situations, so I welcomed this mess with open arms. Some call it desperation, I call it curiosity.

I would think this is very similar to divers who "like" to swim with sharks- they get a rush from it, but ultimately know there is a good chance they will get eaten alive. Is it really worth it?

The annoyance we had for one another made us come back for more. That summer we had the pleasure of seeing each other quite often which made things even more interesting. After continuously being around someone, you learn about them- their interests, what makes them tick, what makes them laugh, why they do the things they do. We were letting small misunderstandings get in the way of friendship. Before I knew it we were talking almost every day...and I never could grasp what I was feeling about him. One minute I was laughing until my stomach hurt and the next I wanted to slap him for trying to make basketball jerseys and bathing suit bottoms a fashion trend.

Correct me if I'm wrong, but I feel like when people have an interest in someone they will do whatever they can to find common interests to talk about, to make the conversation last longer, to pretend to care about every trip they took to their childhood summer camp. We do anything in our power to keep things fluid; to keep it interesting so we ourselves seem interesting. Why do we do this? Because we are stupid. Because somewhere along the way of civilization, a desperate, homely lady, most likely wearing a bonnet, advised us all that this is what we were supposed to do to attract the opposite sex: pretend to be someone we aren't.

This was not the case at all with Sebastian. Talking to him became part of my daily routine and not only that, I was one hundred percent myself. He'd pick up what I put down and dished it right back. I loved it. It was never boring or forced; it was sarcastic and witty. Up until that point in my long lived life, I had never met anyone who kept me on my toes like that.

We still kept things pretty casual--friendly and innocent with a splash of flirtation. When we saw each other in public we kept a reasonable distance with sprinkles of small talk or smiles from across the room.

This continued on for a bit until one fine day Sebastian and his roommate had another party to which I attended. To my surprise, Sebastian was yet again canoodling with a random chick I had never seen before. Well, shit. Someone (me) wasn't playing this game correctly.

My thoughts went something like:

Ok, ok. Play it cool. PLAY. IT. COOL.
Do not keep looking over there; do not make eye contact with the enemy
NO. MATTER. WHAT.
He's looking, he's looking!
Smile.
Smile at everything.
It doesn't matter if no one is speaking to you at the moment, just smile dammit
OK stop smiling
You look like an idiot
Why aren't you better trained for this?
Stop looking confused
Where are my friends? How come I cannot find anyone I know in this tiny house?
HELP.
Why aren't you drinking?
Hello vodka, my old friend.

Now listen up. Listen to me. One of the most important things in life is learning how to react quickly to surprising, or shall we say uncomfortable situations. You have to act with class, the right amount of sass, and humor. Being caught off guard is for morons; always be on your toes. Do this and you will win every time.

The entire night went on and we didn't speak. Can you even believe that? Of course I was secretly bummed out; in my mind things were progressing. As disappointed as I was, I knew the facts: we weren't together and he could talk to whomever he wanted. After All, we had never kissed or went on a date and the main source of communication was through text. That is definitely not the recipe for a relationship. For all I know, I could have been catfished the entire time!

Even though I didn't have a leg to stand on, I still thought it was a dick move. Who spends that much time talking and flirting with someone then turns around to snuggle up to some stranger? Cool bro. Pick one. We are not pieces of candy- you can't have us all.

A princess doesn't chase after men and I wasn't about to start now.

The Almost Lover: Round 2

As you can probably guess, Sebastian didn't quite leave me alone when I tried to keep my distance. I would mentally cut him out and without fail he would break back in. He finally persuaded me to hang out with him one-on-one. I put our differences aside and tried to keep an open mind. It wasn't surprising that our time spent together was charming, but I knew we were headed for dangerous waters.

The Fourth of July rolled around and at this point Sebastian and I had hung out enough times to fill up both hands and hints of romance were starting to blossom. For the longest time we didn't know how to act around each other and not many people knew we were spending time together. At first it was because I had dated Drew and then it was because we had so many mutual friends. There was always a reason why we couldn't just "be."

Anyway, I arrive to the party and tried my hardest to play it cool which essentially meant walking in and not acknowledging him. Like I said before, I am not a smooth person. Eventually he came over and we fell right into our comfortable banter.

In the midst of the get-together I happened to notice he was spending a plentitude of time with what I believe to be a girl. I shit you not, it was hard to tell. What am I chopped liver? What am I doing wrong? SOMEONE EXPLAIN THE ERROR OF MY WAYS! I can't even sit here and talk crap about the other girl because at the end of the day who was the lonely loser in the corner contemplating life itself? Me.

While Sebastian acted like he didn't need to be responsible for his actions, I acted like I wanted no part of his life. I felt like I was his afterthought; the back burner option. I was all set on misreading the signs and feeling like an imbecile.

Before I got all "Gone with the Wind fabulous," I got the courage to let Sebastian know how his thoughtless actions made me feel- I didn't like the game anymore; I was waving the white flag. Nobody has the right to play with people's emotions. Fool me once, shame on you. Fool me twice, well, shame on me.

My little confession seemed to draw him in-he wouldn't go away. I think he needed the verbal validation because after he got it, he couldn't get enough of me. Any outsider would have thought we were a couple, but I didn't have any indication of what he wanted with me- at this point he had to know if he was interested in a relationship or not. Time is of the essence and he was wasting mine. A girl has things to do for crying out loud.

We made plans to hang out again and I came with my own agenda for the evening. I arrived at his house- a sewage smelling "bachelor pad" and thought this was yet another reason I should end things. The stench alone could end my life and I was just too young to die.

An hour and eight minutes had passed before I mustered up the courage to say what was on my mind. A mental battle was taking place within me on whether or not I should just leave things the way they were or find out if there was more; basically trying to convince myself to settle.

What made it worse was that we were arm in arm watching "Never Been Kissed." So I was basically going to deprive us of a perfect, magical evening. Like a polite lady, I waited for a commercial to come on- no one interrupts Drew Barrymore winning prom queen. No one. The words just flew off my tongue, "So I just wanted to know what your thoughts are about us?"

Looking at me with his all-knowing eyes he responded with a sly, "What do you mean?" Typical response. I replayed the words back in my head and wondered what was confusing about them, so I repeated the question slower- as one would do to an elderly, slightly deaf person.

Oh no. I know that look. Prepare for the bullshit.

His speech went something like this:

"Listen, I know we have both thought about this and I know you are frustrated with the situation. I'm just...not looking to get into a relationship right now and honestly, I am in no place to even think about one. There isn't anyone else. You have been my priority as far as women go, if that makes sense, but I can't commit or take on the responsibility of a relationship. I obviously care for you and have a lot of feelings for you, but if you're giving me an ultimatum-whether to grow up and date you or to not have anything- then I guess I am saying not to have anything."

Well that escalated quickly.

I sat there for a moment, trying to get my brain to comprehend the words that were just spoken. Did he just end things? Wasn't I supposed to do that? His response hurt much more than I expected. I kind of felt disposable at that point.

Awkward silence. Awkward Silence. Awkward Silence.

I told him that I was glad he was being honest with me, but I couldn't sit around and wait anymore. I wanted more. I wanted someone to call me theirs. It was becoming apparent that he would never do any of these things no matter what shitty place his life was in. I asked Sebastian what we should do from this point on and he didn't really have the words to make it better. He told me he knew I wasn't happy but that he couldn't give me what I wanted and it would be selfish of him to lie and say he could.

Nothing like kicking someone while they're down.

Like an idiot I started crying-totally embarrassing myself. Sebastian wiped my tears from my face like we were in a corny movie scene. I needed to get out of there immediately before the flood gates opened- a lady simply does not cry in the presence of someone who doesn't deserve her company.

I could tell Sebastian felt terrible and wanted everything that just happened to be permanently erased. He walked me to my car and gave me one of those, ass-out, pat on the back hugs and I drove away without looking back.

I'm not ashamed to admit I cried the entire way home. It's much more dramatic to cry while driving-especially at night with some rain tapping on the windshield. I was disappointed, but also relieved to know the answer about our relationship. In a way I felt freed and knew that I deserved more...much more (accompanied by a couple pints of Ben & Jerry's).

The rendezvous was over...at least for a little while.

I made my departure to test the waters elsewhere. I hadn't been taking my single role as seriously as I should. I needed live it up and make mistakes (because apparently I didn't think I made enough yet). It was time to livin' la vida loca, baby.

So that's what I did.

"A woman is helpless only when her nails are drying."
-Unknown

The Underachiever

There were some non-important life events that took place between me keeping my distance from Sebastian, to meeting basic number four, Mark. I was going out a lot and crying at the fact that the dating world was actually hell on earth. You know when people tell you, "There are plenty of fish in the sea?" That is a lie. The only sea you get to swim in is the Dead Sea.

I now reached a point in my life where I was desperate for a relationship-I wanted nothing more. Being single is fun for a limited time and then it just turns into loneliness. It had been **years** since my breakup with Drew and I was ready to be rescued. Somebody: pick me, love me, choose me! Like, where is my carriage, it should have arrived by now.

The fact that I would have dated just about anyone at this point wasn't a big deal really. I was just on my own personal downward spiral to rock bottom. My frame of mind was clouded and the second someone of potential showed up, I sent my inhibitions to the wind and jumped a little too quickly. Actually scratch that, I didn't just jump, I freakin' leapt...

Meet Mark.

Mark happened to be the older brother of one of my best friends. They were roommates and his house was conveniently two minutes away from where I lived. For whatever reason, my friend had the brilliant idea of getting her brother and me together and at the time, the situation seemed pretty ideal: I got to see Mark, who was definitely cute, and also hang out with my best friends all the time. It was a two for one kind of deal, a buy one get one free.

My first encounter with Mark lasted approximately five minutes. He was extremely drunk and I was the awkward elephant in the room. I was so thankful my two girlfriends were there because he didn't speak to me and I'm almost sure he refused to look me in the eyes...like I was fucking Medusa.

Ok. That went well. Things seem promising.

Second encounter: Once again I was at his house with my friend and he was so nervous that he barely spoke five words to me. The. Entire. Time.

Am I the plague?

Third encounter: A group of us decide to go out, Mark and his sister included. I figured this would create a more comfortable environment for everyone. I summoned the liquid courage to enter my body at once and Mark must have done the same because he shockingly decided to speak and I'll be damned, the conversation turned out to be pretty decent.

Touchdown. He's not a mute.

After that night we graduated from grammar school and were able to successfully hang out by ourselves. After a few dates, I opened my eyes and BAM! I had myself a real life boyfriend. Look mom, he's a real boy! Everything happened rather quickly, which was mistake number one. I wanted something to work so badly and for about one week this seemed to fit. Mark was my "Mr. Right Now," not my "Mr. Right."

So, alright...maybe I didn't know much about him other than he was cute and nice to me. Who cares? He can still be my boyfriend.

What initially intrigued me about Mark was that he had a gentle soul. He was kind and simply wanted to get along with people. I needed kind. I needed gentle. He complimented me all the time and one of my most favorite qualities about him was when I had something to say, he genuinely listened. At least he acted like he did?

In my eyes things couldn't have been better. Maybe this was because I dominated most of the relationship. I could have said I wanted to watch every single episode of every single season of Gossip Girl three times over and he would let me without complaining. Match made in heaven... we were going to get along just fine. Or maybe it was because he made me dinner almost every night. You feed me, I will love you. It's really that simple- just put the food in my face.

While the food never got old, there were plenty of things that did. Come to find out, Mark was a homebody to the most literal meaning. The dude never left his house; sometimes never even left his pajamas. Unfortunately he had been laid off from his job (of course) when we got together so this made things even worse. I probably should have been a tad concerned at this point- seeing as we never went out anywhere. Our dates consisted of me driving to his house, sitting on the couch watching movies and having wine. While I am a sucker for those kinds of evenings, I do enjoy an occasional night out into civilization. This wasn't the apocalypse, so I am not clear on why we couldn't be around other human beings.

We finally made plans one weekend to spend the day at the zoo and I couldn't have been more excited to be doing something active together. It had been so long since I visited the animal exhibits and convince myself they were speaking to me with their eyes.

The morning of our zoo adventure arrived and I called Mark to see what time he wanted to head out. No answer. I assumed he was still sleeping; after all it was only 11am. I patiently waited ten whole minutes before I tried again. No answer. Not a problem, he is bound to wake up in the next five minutes.

Over an hour goes by and I had now turned into one of the caged animals that we had planned on seeing. Mark finally called me around one in the afternoon (prime time at the zoo); completely hung-over to the point he could barely move. Really, man?

Now I am a Christian and I love me some Jesus, but the whole "Thou shalt not kill" thing was about to be thrown to the wind. The crazy bitch had arrived.

I waited a couple hours, for his sake, before I went to his house. With claws out, I pounced into the house ready to attack only to find a present sitting on the table. Aren't we the clever one? I'll give it to him, it was a smart move-I didn't think he had that in him. I put my anger on the shelf for a second and opened the bag before saying hello. As infuriated as I was, the gift was a cute form of an apology. On the table there were flowers along with a stuffed lion and elephant and a note that said "since we can't go to the zoo, I decided to bring the zoo to you! I am sorry."

I found this to be a tricky situation. He was trying to Jedi mind trick me into thinking he performed an adorable act, when in reality he screwed up royally. How do you get hung-over to the point where you can't take your amazing new girlfriend to the zoo? You are a full grown adult and this should definitely not be happening in your life. Get it together.

But surprise, surprise his sorcery worked- he knew that I would fall for any romantic gesture. I still think it was his sister who went out and got these gifts, but whatever I'll let it slide.

Unfortunately, there was no act of romance big enough to keep this relationship alive. The more we got to know each other, the more I realized we had very little in common. I became that girl who tried to mold her boyfriend into the man she wanted him to be. Nothing is more maddening than being that girl. It's like telling the other person, "Never change who you are, except change everything about you." I was literally creating to-do lists for his life.

Knowing we wanted none of the same things in life, my dumbass tried to move forward with the thought that maybe we were just working out the kinks of a newer relationship. I had the bright idea of introducing him to my family as if that would bring us closer together-seemed legit at the time.

Meeting the family wasn't really the bonding experience I had envisioned. It was as if Mark had been violently ripped away from his natural habitat and placed into an experimental cell unit-like where they do tests on rats. The entire situation was painfully awkward; so awkward that at one point I looked up to the heavens and whispered, "Just take me. I am ready."

I come from a large family who is extremely close and social, so when you bring me into your life, you are bringing my family as well. He was a hermit crab who had no interest in social activities or being involved with family...we were doomed.

Houston we have a mother fucking problem.

The ship finally sank on Christmas Eve. You know things are bad when you have no choice but to break up with someone on the most wonderful holiday of the year. Remember when Christmas was a time of peace, love, and joy? Not that year—it was the nightmare before Christmas as I knew it.

What put me over the edge was the fact that Mark, my boyfriend, committed to Christmas Eve dinner at my parents' house with the rest of my extended family. I had a glimpse of hope that things were looking up and he was finally putting in some effort, but do you think Mark showed up? Nope. He informed me a mere two hours before dinner that he would not be coming. The guy didn't even try to make up an excuse. I'll tell you what, the Grinch didn't steal Christmas -Mark did.

I was stunned. That is the best way to put it. I couldn't be in that relationship for one more second so after we had the conversation about him ditching, I immediately called him back and broke up with him. He knew it was coming and, quite frankly, he deserved it.

There were two upsides to this situation:

One: I got to eat my feelings in Christmas food (is there anything better than a home-cooked holiday meal when you are feeling blue?)

Two: I didn't have to break a sweat trying to wrap his presents.

Mark left me alone after the breakup which was a wise decision. I never said he was a stupid man. Finally I learned that it is better to be alone than to settle for less than you deserve.

I got lonely. Mark was there and seemed great in the beginning so I went for it. This was just another stepping stone I needed to walk across. I needed to figure out what I was really looking for in a partner. It's not that Mark was a bad guy or anything-he means well and has a good heart-but we had nothing in common. I needed someone to challenge me; to challenge my thoughts. How we even lasted four months is something to marvel at.

Not to mention we never ended up going to the zoo, ever.

"Sometimes you just need to take a nap and get over it."
-Maura Stuard, Age 8

Houdini

Back into the deep, dark woods I went and while I was in there, I met my own version of the big bad wolf.
You know him: he wants you, charms you, and pursues you. At first you are hesitant; unsure if he is worth your time and unsure if he will ever stop being a douche. After a while you give in and realize things could be worse, with much worse people. A little more time goes by and you've met no one else so you start thinking, "yea I could be into this." You start to reciprocate the feelings and everything is going superb until he mysteriously vanishes from earth itself.

Unfortunately, this is you for the next few days:

"Hello?"

"Are you there? "

"Are you ok? Is everything ok? "

"...so why aren't you answering me? "

"Did I do something wrong or are you upset with me? "

"Did you get abducted?"

"Are you stuck in a zombie apocalypse?"

"Did you lose your hands in a tragic accident and can no longer hold a phone?"

"Have you died and gone to heaven because I now have feelings for you?"

"Did you eat a poisonous apple and fall asleep for one hundred years... hence the reason you cannot respond to me?"

"ARE YOU FUCKING THERE? "

"K."

"Literally done with this. I have zero time for this. You are dead to me"

This is that guy. This is Milo.

I have to make this side comment real quick. I have changed the names of each of my "frogs" for privacy purposes (but you know who you are) and for some reason the name I chose for this one was Milo. If you are weird like me, then you forever and always associate the name Milo with the 1998 horror flick cleverly titled, Milo. The movie is about a pre-teen serial killer (in like grade school) who constantly rides around town on a bicycle and says things to little girls like, "hop on, sugar" in an ultra-creepy kid voice.

I want to make it known that this guy was, in no way, a serial killer and I am fairly certain he isn't one now. I am not writing from the grave.

I first met Milo back in high school and we had a very long, serious four month relationship. He had that funny, yet boyishly charming type of personality, which is what intrigued me. Any boy with charm was a national treasure in my book. The fact that Milo had no shame in showing his feelings for me and pursued me was an even bigger turn on.

My seventeen year old self swooned over the way Milo asked me to be his girlfriend. It was after school and he caught up with me at my locker. We were chatting down the hallway per usual when he whipped out a single rose and handed it to me. The boy had some game. A rose? Are you serious? What seventeen year old sap would say no to that?

We all know the drill...things start out great and for two weeks everything boyfriend does is the cutest thing your eyes will ever see. Quoting movie lines was our favorite hobby and the laughs were endless. We could have fun without even trying and the fact that he was cute, athletic, and a good kisser didn't hurt either. But, like most high school relationships, the cuteness wears off and you realize boyfriend is actually kind of annoying and a bit of an egotistical drama queen- Kanye West style. That is more dramatic than me...and that is no easy feat.

This was high school though, so is anything ever reasonable or mature?

You know those kids who think they personally have a lot of money because their parents do well financially? Milo was one of those kids. I just don't get it; did you earn that money? No. Do you have a secret full time job that we didn't know about? No. Do you think that just because your parents still spoon feed you and give you nice things that you can brag about it? No. We would literally go out to dinner and he would talk about his nice car and would tell me to order whatever I want, he's got it. I understand he was trying to impress me, but c'mon. You are like sixteen, not a sugar daddy and I am pretty sure you still bring a lunch box to school so we can just stop. Please thank your dad for dinner- from the both of us. The pasta was lovely. So were the breadsticks.

I had like a four month dating period with guys in high school. As soon as the fourth month hit, I flipped a switch and wanted out as soon as possible-the same thing was happening with Milo. Instead of letting this drag on any further, I did the mature thing and broke up with him.

It was a Saturday afternoon and I pulled the ol' "let's get together so we can talk" move. He knew what was coming and we were both dreading the awkward situation we would soon find ourselves in. I met him at his parent's house and tried to engage in small talk to take some of the pressure off.

Milo suggested that we rent a movie, clearly a plan to delay the breakup.

Oh no. Just do it. Spit it out. Wow you are really going to Blockbuster right now.

Alright so my initial plans had a wrench thrown into them. To my surprise we were still dating and picking out movies. I let him choose because I have a kind heart, but didn't pay because he needed to know the importance of tough love.

I looked to see what movie Milo had in his hand and then immediately contemplated throwing my own body through the glass window.

Milo picked a little film called, The Aviator. Jiminy fucking cricket. Out of all the movies in the entire store, he had to pick one of the longest movies ever made?! It's THREE HOURS LONG. I was being punished for something I did in my past life, I was sure of it. Not even the beautiful Leonardo DiCaprio playing a pilot was going to change my mind.

Forty minutes had passed and I couldn't take it anymore. I broke the silence with that poignant line we all know from the breakup playbook: "Listen, we need to talk." As to be expected he was upset. Realizing you are losing the best thing that will ever happen to you (me) can be quite devastating.

The truth is I hated being in this position; being the cause of sadness and hurt in someone's life is the last thing I want, but I wasn't happy. I knew it wasn't fair to string him along the rest of my senior year when my intentions were to go off to college as a single woman.

Milo was able to pull himself together and accept the reality of our breakup. We continued to see each other at school and stayed friends, which was nice. I enjoyed him as a person and, in all seriousness, wanted him to be happy.

Fast forward a couple years and Milo snuck his ass back into my life. To be honest, I was not into this idea at all. I was supposed to be meeting strangers in college and bumping into my soul mate at any second. I didn't want a repeat. I always thought of myself as a one and done kind of gal.

But then I got to thinking- the good ones hurt you, the bad ones hurt you, and all the ones in between hurt you too. Milo was the other guy: The guy who always likes you and wants to be with you. The guy who would take any chance he got to be around you. The guy who would treat you like a queen if he were to date you.

It all happened in the summer; he was home from college and asked to hang out, which wasn't out of the ordinary. We met for drinks with two mutual friends and I don't know if it was the alcohol seeping into my bloodstream, but it was like I was seeing him for the first time. Maybe he seemed more grown up or maybe I was ready for a new start with someone, but my body was ready. He caught me off guard by publicly asking me out on an "official date."

Impressive.
Ballsy.
Bold.

I liked it. It seemed devastatingly romantic, like the way Noah made Allie go out on a date with him in front of all those people at the carnival...minus the life-threatening situation.

#Chivalryforlife

After our second "first date, "things started to progress and we became romantically reacquainted. I dealt with some internal, emotional battles in the beginning because I didn't know if I was just lonely and filling my time, or if I truly had an interest in Milo...again. I was remembering the immature, high-schooler who I didn't even take to my own Senior Ball (yes, he was my boyfriend at the time and I went with another friend).

I also pondered why I was recycling old boyfriends and not meeting anyone new. *Is something wrong with me?* Milo seemed different in all the right ways. Within the five seconds of hanging out with him again, he seemed more mature, responsible, and confident in what he wanted in life, so I took it and ran with my fingers crossed the entire way.

As usual, I threw all my inhibitions to the damn wind and off they went. There is a reason why people never say "the second time's the charm." And I am here to tell you why.

Milo was going to college about an hour away from home and wanted me to visit for the night. Of course I agreed, like, hello, I was desperate. To put it briefly: we went out for some drinks, held hands, and talked about life- a nice date if you ask me. I am certain he thought other activities were going to take place, but the milk I was selling wasn't free. Just because I stayed at his place didn't mean mama was opening the cookie jar. Devastation and slight irritation fell across his face when he realized he was being shut down. He respected my wishes, as he should, but I could hear the cries escaping from his soul.

Regardless of the disappointment from the night before, we woke up with smiles and the mood was positive. I liked to think I was pretty good at reading a person's emotions and I couldn't have been more confident that things were in a great place when I left that morning.

Perhaps there was a full moon or my "people reading skills" were complete and utter shit, but I was quickly made aware that things were not in a great place. In fact, things were not in any place. I didn't ask for a magic trick, but he disappeared into thin air anyway. Literally vanished.

This is where those neurotic texts in the beginning of the chapter chime in.

So many things were running through my head; I had never had this happen to me before. Was his only mission to get into my Express Jeans when I went to visit him? Because let me tell you, those suckers fit like a silk glove; there is no room for anyone in there.

Eventually, Milo resurrected from the dead and literally tried telling me he got "busy." He kept spitting out line after line of rubbish. Sweetheart, I think what happened here is that you confused me for a peasant fool. These little games are unamusing and honestly who has the time.

Let's face it, and as much as I hate saying it, he was just not that into me. I read the book and saw the movie, thank you. If someone is disappearing on you...I think it's safe to say they want nothing to do with you... ever. Truer words have never been spoken.

On his good days, Milo would reach out to me and we briefly talked, but we didn't physically spend time together after that. His temperamental emotions were giving me whiplash and I didn't care enough to think about it anymore.

The moment that really sealed the deal was when he kissed a girl in front of my face. I can't say I was enraged or upset, but I was uncomfortable. We weren't dating...we were barely talking at that point, but it just shocked me. Maybe I think too highly of myself- I just figured he would always be pining for me. Ok, so there is a possibility that I am the one with the ego problem.

My uncomfortable meter was at an all-time high and since the night was coming to a close, I decided to make my way out. As I was saying my goodbyes to friends, I noticed Milo being ever so dramatic-standing by himself, in a corner, wearing a pout that I knew all too well.

Despite him acting like a toddler, I still went over to say goodbye, pretending the tonsil hockey game my eyes had the pleasure of watching earlier didn't faze me in the slightest. All of a sudden Milo started rambling; he was feverish. It reminded me of the part in the Exorcist when the girl starts speaking in weird tongues. His babble went on about how he was pissed at himself for acting like an idiot in front of me and how he messed everything up.

Actually Milo, you messed it up when you vanished into thin air but this didn't really help your case either.

The most amusing part was listening to him profess that I was his "ideal, perfect girl who he wanted to end up with." He wished so badly that he was done with college because apparently you cannot pursue a girl while attending school. "I just don't feel good enough about myself to be with you and give you what you need."

Really? Another one who has this line up his sleeve? Is this the first lesson men are taught in life? I knew I was a good catch, but damn, why do these fools keep running in the other direction?

Laughter was my only reaction. Was this boy really expecting me to believe anything when five seconds ago he was eating the mouth off of some chick? Talk is cheap babe and your dream girl is now your worst nightmare, so if you keep talking I will ruin your life.

That was the last push I needed to close Milo's chapter. I guess I always knew deep down that the relationship would never go anywhere- I trusted the little hope I had left but in the end another one bit the dust.

And so there I was again, the lonely rider- back on my quest for love or at least something similar.

The Almost Lover: Round 3 (yes this is still going on)

There must have been some sort of solar eclipse or paradigm shift because Sebastian came back in full swing when he realized how much he missed me. It was as if Satan rose up from the depths of hell and said, "Let there be feelings." I had every intention of running in the other direction but he knew exactly how to pull me right back in and down the rabbit hole we went. I honestly had no clue what I was getting myself into, but everything had changed.

I was not advanced enough for this.

With the blink of an eye, he went from being an acquaintance, to someone I wanted to strangle with his sweaty basketball jersey, to one of my best friends, and then, of course, to an almost lover.

A day didn't pass where we didn't talk to each other all day or hang out. It was becoming a bad habit neither of us wanted to break.

I loved the playfulness of it all; the sneaked kisses when no one was looking, the texting from different rooms at a party, and the stolen glances. It was the way his arms snaked around my waist as if to say "never leave." He was my spirit animal. We told each other everything-shared all our hopes and dreams. I'll never forget the time we passed a jewelry store while walking through the mall- he looked at me and said, "What would you do if I just proposed to you right now?" I laughed it off and called him crazy, but his statement gave me butterflies. Was he finally opening the door to a real relationship together? Has he really thought about marrying me before? My heart was smiling that day.

Sebastian was the only person who could tell me I looked like a dyke when I cut my hair and then immediately kiss me after or show no hesitation in letting me know I was acting like a raging bitch and needed to sit one out. He would email and text me poems just for fun and willingly offered to play the Twilight board game with me on Saturday nights.

Never in my life had I been so comfortable with someone. Sebastian was the Yin to my Yang and the whole cheese to my macaroni thing; he was my best friend. I could never find anyone that could mentally compete with me until he came around. He challenged my thoughts, sparked my creativity, and allowed me to step outside the tiny box I often kept myself in. We were connected on a deeper level which is why it was so hard to put those years behind lock and key.

It was a fun, unordinary ride, but there was never a destination. In my head we were a couple; we did all the things couples do, so you could imagine my humiliation when I once again asked the big "what are we" question and was shut down yet again. Sebastian could not commit. Whatever his excuses were this time I wouldn't allow myself to hear it. Love knows no boundaries and there were many boundaries here.

I was so salty about the entire situation; all my eggs had been placed in his basket and what did I get out of it? I got a cracked shell and a broken heart. I had been giving all my attention and affection to a person who was not worthy of it. I put in work for this man and did my time-I was even accepting of the fact that his ass did not own any form of transportation. Yea, you read that right- on top of everything else I was a personal chauffeur. What am I supposed to do with that, put it on my resume? Over my dead, pasty body was I going to accept this.

Emotionally spent and fed up, I asked myself the question I had continued to dodge: why are you setting? I knew better, I was raised better, and I deserved better. I was so good at being selfish, so what was my problem? I figured that if someone had a problem with me putting myself first, then they needed to get the hell out of my way.

My Fairy Godmother was teaching me a lesson. I had to figure it out for myself and as soon as I did, love finally came looking for me...and this time I was ready.

Before I get into my "happily ever after," let's discuss the demise of the Sebastian saga.

It took meeting the right person for me to let go of what I had, or didn't have, with Sebastian. He was comfortable; he was my safety blanket and I was confusing comfort for love. I stood there, right in front of Sebastian's face for three years. Three fucking years. Our story had become an arduous, drawn out chapter in my life and I needed to turn the page.

Before I met my husband, Sebastian and I were balancing on a landslide-fearful that if we did so much as blink, we would lose it all. There was a ticking time bomb patiently waiting to explode.

Prior to securing a boyfriend, I let Sebastian know I met someone. Out of respect for our friendship, I wanted him to hear that I was pursuing other interests from me. Based on my previous track record, Sebastian had many reasons to believe this was just another failed attempt to move on, but what he didn't know was that I already had.

I am cringing at the fact that Facebook has any sort of part in this story, but the second my status changed from "forever single" to "Hallelujah- in a relationship," shit (and Sebastian) hit the fan.

"I was falling in love with you!" he screamed via Facebook messenger. I found his statement rather intriguing. Shouldn't I have been in the loop on that? Wouldn't I have been aware of this at some point during the three years I had known him? I don't know if he was falling in love with me or just scared of not having me around for his convenience.

I had never seen Sebastian so angry; he had the nerve to tell me I "played him like a fool." Well honey, it takes one to know one. How could this possibly be my fault? He was good at turning tables and messing with my mind, but it wasn't working this time. Sending me a message (not even a phone call or face-to-face-conversation mind you) about how you love me and thought we were already together was a coward's way out. In life you get what you put in and you have to fight for the things you want.

I had to let go of both parts of him. That's the thing about dating your friends- if it doesn't work you lose it all. It's a risk you have to be willing to take. Losing the friend cut the deepest; I knew it was something I would never get back. We chose to cross that barrier that divides friendship and romance and no matter how much we cared for each other or how many times I tried to accept the relationship for what it was, it was never enough. It would never be enough.

This was the way we were. All we needed was Barbara Streisand to show up and start singing to really make it official.

The split was like trying to tear off acrylic nails one by one: painful followed by the understanding that you should never try them again. It was the end of an era.

Almost five years have passed now and Sebastian and I are two strangers living their own lives. By the off chance we bump into one another, which has happened over the years, we share nothing but a distant glance and go our separate ways. All that's left to say is, danke schoen, darling, danke schoen.

"Let love come to you, be patient. In fairy tales they don't find each other until the last page."

-Iliketoquote.com

The Frog Turned Into the Prince

If I couldn't make a man myself, Frankenstein style, then this was the next best thing.

There was a light at the end of my tunnel, praise the good Lord Jesus above. It just kind of happened without expectation or warning- as these things usually do. I was technically still "with" Sebastian, but we were never in an exclusive relationship or any type of established relationship so I was keeping my options open.

I will begin by saying that I didn't have a single ounce of interest in meeting Patrick, my husband. A friend of mine knew him because he was friends with her boyfriend and so of course she wanted to hook us up. When you are single, there seems to be some sort of time frame people have for you before they start playing matchmaker and apparently my time had been maxed out.

It was Patrick's birthday party and selfishly my friend wanted me to come so she had someone to hang out with. I refused. After some pushing, prodding and advising that there would be free drinks, I miserably agreed to go. I always got time for some free drinks.

I didn't pay attention to Patrick; instead I hovered over the bar while staring creepily off into the distance at what looked to be my death sentence. I was getting a refill on my vodka cranberry when Patrick approached me, making a casual joke to break the ice. I looked up (mentally telling myself to play nice) and quickly realized I wasn't the slightest bit annoyed at this handsome, charming person looking at me. I remember thinking he had the prettiest blue eyes and nice broad shoulders. And can you even believe he was a redhead? Talk about stepping out of my comfort zone. Was this me starting to have some fun? My black heart was unsure-it had been awhile. Like a gentleman, Patrick asked me what song I wanted the DJ to play and without hesitation I answered, "Anything Michael Jackson."

Minutes later I hear, "The Way You Make Me Feel" and immediately the blood was pumping through my veins (my sole purpose in life is to dance to MJ music). He took my hand and we tore up the dance floor. With sweat beating down from our foreheads and a circle of bystanders around us, we took leg kicks and hip thrusts to an entirely new level: modern day Dirty Dancing.

The night ended and things were awkwardly left in the air. I actually had plans to hang out with Sebastian the next night, so I wasn't reading too much into anything. I was at Sebastian's house per usual when I received a text from Patrick and I guess you could say I was interested because I spent the majority of the night texting back and forth.

He asked me out and we decided to do a double date with our mutual friends. I remember it like it was yesterday. He showed up and we looked like twins- with our matching colored jackets (soulmate goals).

Being picked up to go on a date was orgasmic to me. Why is this not a standard in today's society? I am all for being an independent woman, but I still believe in some old fashion romance (it's the little things). We hit it off from the start-he seemed mature, confident, and knew exactly what he wanted-that couldn't be any more appealing to me.

Patrick was a man with solid morals, values and a great sense of humor. The fact that we were both equally weird was an added bonus. We dated eight months before we were engaged. It was quick. It was crazy. It maybe wasn't the smartest move, but it was love.

The Proposal

It was the day before Christmas Eve. Stockings were hung, lights strung around the house, and I had already reached my eating quota for the next five years. Patrick and I made plans to go ice skating at an outdoor rink and I couldn't wait for work to be over. Bundled up in our winter gear we laced up our skates (well Patrick did mine because, you know, I am an infant) and made our way out onto the ice. A light snow sprinkled down on our faces and I was in awe at the fact that my body hadn't yet surrendered to the ice. I was becoming Nancy Kerrigan right before my own eyes.

In the midst of our synchronized skating routine, an announcement was made for all skaters to clear the ice so the Zamboni can do its thing. As Patrick and I patiently waited alongside strangers who also decided to brave the ice that evening, the loudspeaker started to play Elton John's "Your Song" (my favorite song-it's everything).

Patrick nudged me and said: "Come with me, let's go skate"

"Uh, did you not put your listening cap on? They said we had to wait until the Zamboni is done."

"Just come with me"

"Absolutely not"

"Take my hand, let's go"

We were the only people on the ice. Embarrassment washed over me as I waited for someone to start yelling at us, but it never happened.

All of a sudden our mutual photographer friend popped out of some bushes and started taking pictures of us. My first thought was Patrick arranged a holiday portrait session for the two of us and I thanked myself for actually doing my hair that day. I was down with getting a holiday portrait and feeling like a celebrity.

We continued skating when, from the corner of my eye, I noticed Patrick's dad and sisters standing together in the distance. My stomach instantly flipped. In front of the crowd of mostly strangers we stopped in the middle of the rink- just the two of us, hand in hand. Patrick dropped down to one knee and I began to shake. Our eyes locked and he spoke the words every woman dreams of hearing. This man wanted to spend the rest of his life with me! I know he said some other beautiful things because I saw his mouth moving, but I was so utterly shocked that it's all a blur. A tiny black box peeped its way out of his pocket and inside it held the most breathtaking, sparkly diamond ring I have ever laid eyes on.

Was I dreaming? Was I not just the main character in Les Miserables a year ago? How quickly things can change in the most amazing ways. After my shock wore off I shouted "yes!" and shoved that gorgeous rock onto my finger. This experience, this life changing experience, was a perfect moment in time...and it was all mine.

The next year and a half went by and before I knew it, the twenty sixth of May had arrived: my wedding day. Covered in off-white chiffon along with my something borrowed, new and blue, I felt like a true princess- even better than the Disney ones. Move over bitches, it's my time to shine.

The church doors opened and I charged down that aisle like I was Mel Gibson performing his "freedom yell" in Braveheart. I had officially entered the I-never-have-to-date-again club and could now purchase those his and her pillows without feeling ashamed.

The movies never show you what comes after the big wedding. Marriage is work; it's more than love. Yes, you have the perfect wedding day and ride off into the sunset but then you have every single day after that. It is choosing your battles and compromising. It is about respecting one another and valuing the other's opinions. Most importantly it is being there to support one another and loving them no matter what; no matter how ugly or fat you get. These are the things that make a "happily ever after" and are what my husband and I strive for every day. This is why I know we will truly last forever.

From the moment I laid my eyes on my first Disney movie (Beauty and the Beast if you have retained nothing and forgot already) I wanted my own princess story. All that time I was searching for my very own prince and with a bit of God's humor along the way, I found something better. And you know what's even funnier? My husband literally looks like the prince from Beauty and the Beast (if he grew out his hair)...the one I cried about.

"The love we were promised in fairy tales was never something for us to find. It has always been something for us to create."
-Tyler Kent White

Afterthoughts

As I was sitting here trying to wrap this up, it all started to make sense. I once took a truth-telling BuzzFeed quiz titled, "Which Greek Goddess Are You?" and received the result of "You are Hera, Queen of the Goddesses." I now understand why these men could never make the jump for me. Sorry guys! I didn't realize I was the queen supreme.

Man I feel so much better now.

In my wiser years I have learned the following:

- We make our own fairytales
- Mice take much longer than anticipated to train. I am still waiting for them to sew me a gown but they are underperforming.
- My husband is my very own Prince Charming and to prove it he calls me princess every day to appease me (also gives me treats to make me love him more and it works)
- My castle is anywhere my husband and I decide to call home
- The love for myself comes first, above all, always

- And most importantly, what I came to realize is that my favorite Disney Princess is me (and I will continue to refer to myself as one because life is much more entertaining that way)

We are humans; we are built to fail and get up again. What I can say for certain is that at the end of the day, when it comes to the matters of the heart, we get to choose. We choose who to love, how to love, and who to be loved by (with the hopes that there is at least one person for the job). It doesn't get any better than that.

Unfortunately there comes a time where we go for the cheaters, the missing links, the almost lovers, the underachievers, and the Houdini's-it's only natural. But wouldn't life be such a bore if we didn't? Mistakes are meant to add some color to these short-lived adventures we call life. Who would be able to laugh at our pain and learn from our gain if we did things right the first time? Think about all the stories we would miss out on!

The journey was never about finding love, it was about finding myself. The things I have learned and the experiences that have scarred me for life are what made me into the fabulous woman I am today, so ultimately I owe myself a thank you.

When I look back on it all, I have no regrets. We are in charge of our story-every single step of the way. Some of these relationships were a lot of fun and with people I wish nothing but the best for and others came straight from the place where nightmares are made of, but I figured I would share my stories because everyone's been there at least once and we can all laugh together and hug.

After all, there is nothing wrong in flirting with frogs.

About the Author

Maxie Marcell is a first time author, but an experienced daydreamer. She resides in Rochester, NY with her husband and the rest of her family. When she isn't eating, or thinking about eating, you can find her spending time with the people she loves (which usually also involves eating)...and dancing to Michael Jackson.